FlyHigh
Pupil's Book

3

Jeanne Perrett   Charlotte Covill

Contents

THE FLY HIGH BAND

Hello, girls and boys! 🎵

Hello, girls and boys,
Hello to you.
We are the animals in the zoo.
We're your friends and we are here.
We're learning English all the year.

Hello, girls and boys,
Hello to you.
We're your friends here in the zoo.
We like songs and books and fun.
Let's learn English, everyone!

Hello, girls and boys,
Hello to you.
Welcome to our zoo!

1   **Write the names.**

1

 Africa
 airport
 aunt
 uncle
 cousin
 holiday

He's from Africa.

It's a beautiful day!

Yes, it is! What's that noise?

It's my mobile phone.

Hello? Ziggy! How are you?

I'm fine, thank you.

I'm at the airport. I'm with my aunt, uncle and cousin. We're coming to the zoo.

Ziggy is here on holiday.

Hooray! Ziggy is my friend. He's a zebra. He's from Africa!

1 **Circle.**

1 What's the noise?   (A mobile phone.) / A radio.
2 Where's Ziggy?   In Africa. / At the airport.
3 Who's with Ziggy?   His aunt, uncle and cousin. / Sally and Trumpet.
4 Where's Ziggy going?   To the zoo. / To the airport.
5 Where's Ziggy from?   The zoo. / Africa.

Learn with Tag

I am → I'm
You/We/They are → You/We/They're
He/She/It is → He/She/It's

2 **Listen and stick.**

Taras   Rosa   Elizabeth

3 **Circle and write.**

1 Taras is from England / Ukraine. His flag is _____blue_____ and _____ .
2 Rosa is from Ukraine / Argentina. Her flag is _____ , _____ and _____ .
3 Elizabeth is from Argentina / England. Her flag is _____ , _____ and _____ .

4 **What about you? Write.**

I'm from _____ . My flag is _____ .

5 **Sing along with the FlyHigh band!**

Let's dance!
I'm from England,
He's from France,
We're from Greece,
Come on, let's dance.
Play and laugh, boys and girls.
You're the children of the world.
Where are you from? Where are you from?
Let's all dance and sing this song.
Where are you from? Where are you from?
Let's all dance and sing this song.

2

 shy
 England
 spaghetti
 cheese
 ice cream
 dinner

Are you on holiday?

(1) **Match.**

1 She isn't shy.   **2** They're on holiday.   **3** They're hungry.   **4** She's tired.

 **a**

 **b**

 **c**

 **d**

Learn with Tag

Are you?	I'm not.
Am I?	You aren't.
Is he/she/it?	He/She/It isn't.
Are we/you/they?	We/You/They aren't.

2 **What about you? Write.**

1 Is your mum a dancer? ....
2 Is your dad a police officer? ....
3 Are your friends funny? ....
4 Is your grandpa tall? ....
5 Are your aunt and uncle teachers? ....

3 **Play the game.**

cowboy spy
lion
giant kangaroo
frog duck
clown
monkey

4 **Write with Karla.**

My name is Karla.
I'm nine years old.
I'm from Australia.
My flag is red, white and blue.

My name is ....
....
....
....
....
....

3

 map
 shorts
 sunglasses
 shirt
 swimsuit
 smile

I've got a camera.

1 **Choose and write.**

swimsuit   map   ~~clothes~~   shorts

1 Ziggy has got lots of new ___clothes___ .
2 They've got a _____ of Turkey.
3 Ziggy has got black and white _____ .
4 His cousin has got a new _____ .

I've got a camera.
She's got sunglasses.

Learn with Tag

I/You/We/They have got → I/You/We/They 've got
He/She/It has got → He/She/It's got

2 **Write.**

1 I / 2 /

I've got two swimsuits.

2 She / 20 /

3 They / 12 /

4 He / 5 /

3 **Read and write. Then colour.**

I've got beautiful clothes. My T-shirt is the colour of bananas. My skirt is the colour of the sea. My shoes are the colour of chocolate. My sunglasses are the colour of a swan.

1 She's got a ....yellow........ T-shirt.
2 She's got a .... skirt.
3 She's got .... shoes.
4 She's got .... sunglasses.

4 **Sing along with the FlyHigh band!** ♫

Lucky girls and boys

We've got books and bags and pens.
We've got family and we've got friends.
We've got bikes and lots of toys.
We are very lucky girls and boys.
We are very lucky girls and boys.

We've got houses and we've got warm beds.
We've got shoes and hats for our heads.
We've got games and we've got toys.
We are very lucky girls and boys.
We are very lucky girls and boys.

4

 passport   ticket   plane   money   suitcase   taxi

Have you got your passports?

1   **Circle.**

1   The zebras have got their plane tickets.   yes / no
2   Chatter has got their money.   yes / no
3   There's a taxi for the zebras.   yes / no
4   Sally has got a surprise for the animals.   yes / no
5   Sally has got a box of toys.   yes / no

Have I got my camera?
I haven't got my camera.

Learn with Tag

Have I/you/we/they got?
Yes, I/you/we/they have.
No, I/you/we/they haven't.

Has he/she/it got?
Yes, he/she/it has.
No, he/she/it hasn't.

2 **What about you? Circle and write.**

1 Have / **Has** your friend got a dog? ....
2 Have / Has you got a bike? ....
3 Have / Has your teacher got a black car? ....
4 Have / Has you got a blue bag? ....

3 **Listen and match.**

1 Has Sandy got a grey computer?   **a** Yes, he has.
2 Has she got a pink mobile phone?   **b** Yes, she has.
3 Has Paul got a green bike?   **c** No, she hasn't.
4 Has he got a camera?   **d** No, he hasn't.

4 **Play the game.**

Have you got a green cat?

No, I haven't!

Maths

English

(1) Read and answer.

1 Has Joanna got her Maths, English and History books? ..... Yes, she has.
2 Has Joanna got a pet? .....
3 Is it Wednesday? .....
4 Has Joanna got Art on Tuesday? .....
5 Has Joanna got English on Wednesday? .....

History
 Art
 dinosaur
 PE

5

Art. Draw a picture of your pet! Oh, no!

6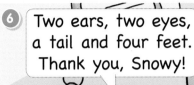

Two ears, two eyes, a tail and four feet. Thank you, Snowy!

That's not me!

7

It's Tuesday today! We haven't got Art. We've got PE.

Oh, no! I haven't got my shorts!

8

I've got two beautiful green eyes, two big ears, a long tail and four pretty feet. I'm a lovely cat!

2 **Write with Karla.**

I've got a small family. I've got a mum, a dad and one sister. I've got an aunt and an uncle, but I haven't got a cousin. My sister is shy. I'm not shy.

I've got ....

....

....

....

....

....

The FlyHigh Review ①

1 Match.

1 My aunt and uncle are on holiday.
2 My aunt is on holiday.
3 My uncle is on holiday.
4 My cousin and I are on holiday.
5 You and your family are on holiday.

a He's on holiday.
b You're on holiday.
c They're on holiday.
d We're on holiday.
e She's on holiday.

2 Read and answer.

1 Are cherries grey?   No, they aren't.
2 Is a butterfly an insect?
3 Are whales big?
4 Are penguins green and white?
5 Is milk red?
6 Are carrots orange?

3 Write.

A

B

1 He's got ......a camera...... .
2 ....
3 ....

4 They've got ....
5 ....
6 ....

4 What about you? Write.

1 Have you got a mobile phone? ....
2 Have you got a computer? ....
3 Has your cousin got a bike? ....
4 Has your grandma got a dog? ....
5 Have your aunt and uncle got a white car? ....

5 Listen and circle.

Monday	Tuesday	Wednesday	Thursday	Friday
History / (English)	Maths / English	PE / Art	History / Maths	PE / English
PE / Maths	Art / History	English / History	Art / PE	Maths / Art

Now write She's got **or** She hasn't got.

1 ___She's got___ English on Monday.
2 .... Art on Tuesday.
3 .... Maths on Wednesday.
4 .... PE on Thursday.
5 .... History on Friday.

My Project   Draw and make a holiday chart. Then write.

Me	My friend
– green shorts	– blue sunglasses
– a blue book	– a purple swimsuit
– a camera	– a map
– a passport	– train tickets

In my holiday bag, I've got green shorts and a blue book.
I've also got a camera and my passport. My friend has got
blue sunglasses and a purple swimsuit. She's also got a map
and train tickets.

Now go to
**My Picture
Dictionary**

5

morning	letter	postcard	parcel	afternoon	evening	watch TV

The postman comes at seven.

1 **Circle.**

1 The postman comes at six.   yes / no

2 There's a parcel for Sally.   yes / no

3 The postcard is from Chatter.   yes / no

4 Ziggy swims in the evening.   yes / no

5 Chatter opens the parcel.   yes / no

They play games.

Learn with Tag

I/You/We/They play games.
He/She/It plays games.

2 **Circle and write.**

1 Sally get up / (gets up) at .... six ....

2 Rob and Vicky go / goes to school at ....

3 The zoo open / opens at ....

4 The shops close / closes at 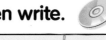 ....

3 **Listen and stick. Then write.**

1 In the morning we ....
2 In the afternoon we ....
3 In the evening we ....
4 At night I ....

4 **Sing along with the FlyHigh band!** ♫

Lucky Ziggy

Lucky, lucky Ziggy
Every day, he plays.
Lucky, lucky Ziggy
He's on holiday.

Lucky, lucky Ziggy
Every day, he plays.
Lucky, lucky Ziggy
He's on holiday.

He plays on the beach.
He swims in the sea.
He eats an ice cream.
He watches TV.

6

 photo album

 weekend

 ski

 year

 mountain

 winter

 summer

Do they play basketball?

---

1 **Choose and write.**

year   weekend   ~~photo album~~   winter

1 Sally has got a new .... photo album ....

2 Her friends watch basketball every ....

3 Her family skis every ....

4 They go to the mountains in ....

I/You/We/They don't play basketball.

Do you play basketball?　Yes, I do. / No, I don't.
Yes, we do. / No, we don't.

Do they play basketball?　Yes, they do. / No, they don't.

2　**What about you? Circle.**

1　We read / don't read at school.
2　I walk / don't walk to school.
3　We have lunch / don't have lunch at school.
4　I do my homework / don't do my homework in my bedroom.
5　My friends play / don't play football in the park.

3　**Play the game.**

I do this every weekend.

No, I don't.

Do you play football?

Do you dance?

Yes, I do.

4　**Write with Karla.**

My holiday
I'm on holiday in the mountains with my family.
In the morning we ski.
In the afternoon we play games.
In the evening we write postcards.

My holiday
I'm on holiday ....
In the morning ....
....
....

7

 meat
 excited
 panda
 China
 leaf

She doesn't like meat.

1 It's Saturday. Everyone is excited. There's a new animal at the zoo.

Wow! A panda.

Her name's Pandora.

She's very sweet. How old is she?

Does she come from Africa?

She's three.

No, she doesn't. She comes from China.

2 What does she eat?

She eats leaves. She doesn't like meat.

Does she sleep a lot?

Yes, she does. She sleeps all the time.

3 Look!

Hello, Pandora.

1 **Choose and write.**

eats   comes from   ~~is~~   sleeps

1 Pandora _____ is _____ a panda.
2 She _____ China.
3 Pandora _____ leaves.
4 She _____ a lot.

Does he eat meat?
Yes, he does.

He/She/It doesn't eat meat.

Does he eat meat?   Yes, he does. / No, he doesn't.
Does she eat meat? Yes, she does. / No, she doesn't.
Does it eat meat?   Yes, it does. / No, it doesn't.

2 **Choose and write. Use** doesn't.

eat   wear   ~~come from~~   go   play

1 Ziggy .... doesn't come from .... China.
2 Pandora .... meat.
3 Vicky .... to school on Saturday.
4 Chatter .... the guitar.
5 Trumpet .... sunglasses.

3 **Read and answer.**

This panda comes from China. Its favourite food is bamboo leaves. It doesn't sleep all winter.

1 Does the panda come from Africa? .... No, it doesn't.
2 Does it come from China? ....
3 Does it eat leaves? ....
4 Does it sleep all winter? ....

4 **Sing along with the FlyHigh band!** ♫

Pandora likes the zoo.
Does Pandora like the zoo?
Yes, she does.
Does she like me and you?
Yes, she does. Yes, she does.
She likes me and you.

Does Chatter like the zoo?
Yes, he does.
Does he like me and you?
Yes, he does. Yes, he does.
He likes me and you.

8

 wake up

 early

 show

 bird

 late

 want

They always wake up early.

1. On Sunday Patty shows Pandora the zoo.

I live here with my family. We live next to the birds. They always wake up early. They never get up late.

2. This is the playground.

We sometimes play here in the afternoon.

Here's Chatter.

3. This is Trumpet. He has a shower every day.

4. Oh, dear!

I'm fine. This is fun.

I want a shower too!

1 Circle.

1 It's Saturday / Sunday.
2 Patty lives next to the pandas / birds.
3 The birds get up early / late.
4 They go to the playground / park.
5 Trumpet is having breakfast / a shower.

I always clean my teeth.

We sometimes go to the park.
They never eat meat.

always   sometimes   never

Learn with Tag

I clean my teeth in the morning.
We go to the park on Saturday.
They eat bread every day.

2 **What about you? Write** always, sometimes **or** never.

1 I .... clean my teeth in the morning.
2 I .... get up early.
3 I .... eat lunch at school.
4 I .... go to bed at nine.
5 I .... go to school on Sunday.

3 **Listen and match. Then write.**

1 Monday **2** Tuesday **3** Wednesday **4** Thursday **5** every day

a  **b**  **c**  **d**  **e**

1 ....On Monday....... Vicky swims.
2 .... she plays the guitar.
3 .... she goes to the zoo.
4 .... she goes to the playground.
5 .... she plays tennis.

4 **Play the game.**

I wear brown shoes.

always | sometimes | never

I always wear brown shoes.

I sometimes wear brown shoes.

I never wear brown shoes.

Sally's Story
The months of the year

① ## Spring

In March the birds begin to sing.
They are happy now it's spring.

In April blue skies come again.
There's sometimes sun and sometimes rain.

In May it's warm and we can play
Out in the sunshine every day.

② ## Summer

In June the days are hot and bright
And stars shine in the sky at night.

In July we feel so free
Swimming in the bright blue sea.

In August we're on holiday.
Summer is the time to play!

---

① **Read and write.**

1 It sometimes snows in .... January ....
2 The birds begin to sing in ....
3 We swim in ....
4 It's time to go to school in ....
5 The days are dark in ....
6 It's Christmas in ....

April May June July August
November December

③ **Autumn**

In September 'Hello friends!'
It's time to go to school again.

In October yellow leaves
Fall from all the autumn trees.

In November days are dark
And we can't play out in the park.

④ **Winter**

In December Christmas comes.
Fun and games for everyone!

In January it sometimes snows.
The days are short, the cold wind blows.

In February the winter trees
Are black and brown; there are no leaves.

---

② **Write with Karla.**

My favourite season is autumn.
I go to school.
I play in the leaves.
I wear my sweater.

My favourite season is ....

....

....

....

twenty-seven　27

The FlyHigh Review ②

1 **Listen and match.**

spring   summer   autumn   winter

a  **b**  **c**  **d**

Now choose and write.

play   ~~fly~~   feed   wake up

1 The bees ___fly___ in ___summer___ .
2 The zookeeper _____ the birds in _____ .
3 The monkeys _____ with the leaves in _____ .
4 The bear _____ in _____ .

2 **Write.**

1 Rabbits eat meat.   Rabbits don't eat meat.
2 It snows in summer.   _____
3 Pandas come from Africa.   _____
4 The sun shines at night.   _____
5 We live in trees.   _____

3 **What about you? Write Do or Does and answer.**

1 ___Does___ your postman come in the morning? _____
2 _____ you wash your hair every day? _____
3 _____ your dad go home in the afternoon? _____
4 _____ your mum read in the evening? _____
5 _____ your friends go to your house every day? _____

4 Write and colour the boxes. Then play the game.

It's July.

July is in summer.

March   June   December   February
November   September   October   April
July   ~~January~~   May   August

J anuary	F	M	A	M	J
J	A	S	O	N	D

 = spring   = summer   = autumn   = winter

5 What about you? Write.

1 What's your name? ....
2 Where do you come from? ....
3 How old are you? ....
4 When is your birthday? ....

My Project Make a poster.

In spring it's *my* birthday. I have a party.

In summer I go on holiday with my family. I swim in the sea.

In autumn I go to school again, I learn English.

In winter I go to the mountains. I ski in the snow!

Now go to
My Picture Dictionary

1 **Say it with Sally.**

a) **Listen and point. Then repeat.**

k

g

j

x

b) **Listen and write. Then repeat.**

1 fo x

2 itchen

3 uitar

4 elly

5 ump

6 bo

7 angaroo

8 irl

c) **Chant.**

Jumping jellies.   Cakes in the kitchen.   The fox is next to the box.   Tag's got a guitar.

2 **Colour the family members to get to the plane. Then write.**

START	mum	swimsuit	car	spaghetti	train
park	brother	aunt	cousin	shirt	tiger
Maths	zebra	meat	grandma	playground	History
cheese	England	bus	sister	dad	airport
dress	lion	shorts	PE	uncle	grandpa
taxi	ice cream	Art	dinosaur	zoo	

four foods   spaghetti
four kinds of clothes
four places in town
four lessons
four animals
four kinds of transport
Where are the family going?

3 Look and answer.

1 How many planes can you see?	.......2.......
2 How many children can you see?	....
3 How many people have got sunglasses?	....
4 How many suitcases can you see?	....
5 How many people have got a book?	....
6 How many people have got a hat?	....
7 How many maps can you see?	....
8 How many babies can you see?	....
9 How many people have got food?	....
10 How many passports can you see?	....

9

 cook   learn   talk   bored   home   doorbell   ring

I'm cooking.

> Tag is playing his guitar. Karla and Trumpet are learning a new song. Chatter is talking to Rob.

> Hello, Rob. Hello, Vicky. I'm bored.

> I've got an idea. Let's visit Sally.

> Sally is at home.

> Hello. I'm cooking. You can help me.

> Oh, good.

> This is fun.

SUGAR   FLOUR

> Oh, dear. What a mess!

> The doorbell is ringing. Who is it?

---

(1)   **Match.**

1   Tag is   **a**   learning a new song.

2   Karla and Trumpet are   **b**   playing his guitar.

3   Chatter is   **c**   ringing.

4   Sally is   **d**   talking to Rob.

5   The doorbell is   **e**   cooking.

I am cooking. → I'm cooking.
You/We/They are cooking. → You/We/They're cooking.
He/She/It is cooking. → He/She/It's cooking.

! have → having   make → making

2 **Write.**

1 You _____'re learning_____ (learn) English.
2 She _____ (listen) to the radio.
3 I _____ (cook) lunch in the kitchen.
4 We _____ (play) with our friends.
5 The phone _____ (ring).

3 **Listen and stick. Then write.**

1 My dad ____is cleaning____ his teeth.
2 My brother _____ .
3 My mum _____ .
4 My grandma and grandpa

_____ .

4 **Sing along with** the **FlyHigh** band! ♫

Fun in the kitchen
We're cooking in the kitchen.
We are having lots of fun.
We are making a cake
To eat with everyone.

Yum, yum! Yum, yum!
We're eating every crumb!

We're cleaning up the kitchen.
We're having lots of fun.
We are eating the cake.
We're eating every crumb!

10

 make
 wash
 dish
 floor
 strawberry
 taste

You aren't helping.

1 **Circle.**

1 Trumpet, Karla and Patty are looking for Chatter. yes / no

2 Sally, Vicky, Rob and Chatter are making biscuits. yes / no

3 Tag is washing the dishes. yes / no

4 Patty is helping. yes / no

5 The cake is a surprise for Tag. yes / no

I'm not playing basketball.

I am not sleeping. → I'm not sleeping.
You/We/They are not sleeping. → You/We/They aren't sleeping.
He/She/It is not sleeping. → He/She/It isn't sleeping.

❗ taste → tasting

2 **Write** isn't/aren't **+ ... ing.**

drink ~~paint~~ eat make wear

1 George _____isn't painting_____ a rabbit.
2 He _____ milk.
3 Julia _____ a card.
4 She _____ a banana.
5 They _____ new clothes.

3 **Play the game.**

I'm cleaning my teeth. Where am I?

bathroom | bedroom
kitchen | living room

Are you in the bathroom?

Yes, I am.

4 **Write with Karla.**

Me and my friend
I'm in the kitchen.
I'm doing my homework.
Patty is in the living room.
She isn't doing her homework.
She's reading a book.

Me and my friend
I'm in _____ .
_____
_____
_____
_____
_____
_____

11

go shopping

library

cinema

supermarket

buy

rope

Are you going to town?

1   Choose and write.

are making   ~~is going~~   is buying   are going

1 Sally ....is going........ to town.
2 They .... to the supermarket.
3 Sally .... food and a rope.
4 They .... a new swing.

Is he eating?
Yes, he is!

Learn with Tag

Am I eating?	Yes, you are. / No, you aren't.
Are you eating?	Yes, I am. / No, I'm not.
Is he/she/it eating?	Yes, he/she/it is.
	No, he/she/it isn't.
Are we/you/they eating?	Yes, you/we/they are.
	No, you/we/they aren't.

shop → shopping   sit → sitting

2 **Write.**

1 ..... Is ..... the man ..... buying ..... (buy) apples?
..... No, he isn't. .....

2 ..... he ..... (wear) a shirt?

3 ..... the woman ..... (sit down)?

4 ..... they ..... (laugh)?

3 **Look and answer.**

1 Where is the man shopping?   He's shopping in a supermarket.
2 What is he buying?

4 **Sing along with** the FlyHigh band! ♫

Where are you going to?   I'm not going to the toy shop.
Are you going to the toy shop?   I'm not going to the zoo.
Are you going to the zoo?   I'm going to the cinema.
Are you going to the cinema?   Are you coming too?
Where are you going to?

CINEMA

Yes, I'm coming with you.
Yes, I'm coming with you.

12

 wait
 move
 chase
 stop
 thief
 brave

Wait here. Don't move.

(1) **Choose and write.**

police   ~~library~~   thief   animals

1   In picture 1 Sally is going to the ....library........ .
2   In picture 2 the police are chasing the ....
3   In picture 3 Chatter and Trumpet are helping the ....
4   In picture 4 the police officer is talking to the ....

Learn with Tag

Run!

Yes, let's run.

Don't run.

Let us → Let's
Do not → Don't

2 Listen and tick (✓).

1 a ✓ b ✗

2 a b ✗

3 a b ✗

4 a b ✗

3 Circle.

1 It's nine o'clock. Go / Don't go to bed, please.
2 I'm hungry. Let's have / Don't have lunch.
3 Grandma is coming today. Please make / don't make a mess in your room.
4 It's hot in here. Please open / don't open the window.
5 This is a library. Be quiet, / Don't be quiet, please.

4 Play the game.

Sally says 'Dance, please'.

Sally says 'Stop, please'.

Let's sit down.

The bear fight

fight

go for a walk

swing

① Adam! Harry! Where are you?

Are you watching TV?

We're in my bedroom, Grandma!

No, we aren't.

② Good. It's a lovely, sunny day. Let's go for a walk.

Oh, no, Grandma! We're playing!

③ What are you playing?

I'm swinging on a rope and Harry is skiing.

④ What?

We're climbing a mountain now, Grandma.

Are you OK?

① **Read and answer.**

1 Are Harry and Adam in the bedroom? ..... Yes, they are. .....

2 Are they watching TV? .....

3 Is it a sunny day? .....

4 Is Grandma in the kitchen? .....

5 Is she carrying a saucepan? .....

6 Are the boys playing a computer game?

saucepan

⑤ Yes! Harry is chasing a bear!

In your bedroom?

Yes! I'm fighting the bear now!

⑥ Arthur! There's a bear in the bedroom!

Yes. The boys are fighting a bear!

A bear?

⑦ I'm coming, boys! I've got a saucepan! Don't worry!

⑧ We're playing a computer game, Grandpa!

Let's make spaghetti!

---

② **Write with Karla.**

This is a picture of my family.
I'm reading.
My sister is jumping.
My dad is sleeping.

This is a picture of my family.

I'm ....

....

My ....

....

My ....

....

1 Listen and match.

1   2  3  4  5

a  b c  d  e

2 Write Let's or Don't.

1 The kitchen is a terrible mess. _____Let's_____ clean the floor.
2 It's lunchtime. _____ wash our hands.
3 I'm not playing. I'm going shopping. _____ wait for me.
4 There's a butterfly on your shoe. _____ move.
5 It's a windy day. _____ fly the kite.

3 What about you? Choose and write.

We	
I	My teacher
	My friend

learning English
writing on the board   singing
standing up   laughing   listening
sitting down   wearing trousers

1 _____I_____ 'm _____learning English_____ .
2 _____ 'm not _____ .
3 _____ 's _____ .
4 _____ isn't _____ .
5 _____ 're _____ .
6 _____ aren't _____ .

4 Look and say.

making a dress / wearing the dress
looking for the cat / playing with the cat
cleaning the window / opening the window

carrying the TV / watching TV
eating / singing
running / sleeping

In Picture 1 the girl is making a dress.

In Picture 2 the girl is wearing the dress.

My Project Make a class map.

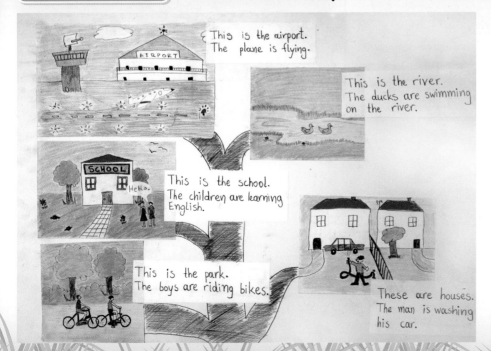

This is the airport. The plane is flying.

This is the river. The ducks are swimming on the river.

This is the school. The children are learning English.

These are houses. The man is washing his car.

This is the park. The boys are riding bikes.

Now go to

My Picture Dictionary

13

 toothbrush

 half past five

 concert

 towel

 shampoo

 argue

He's got my toothbrush.

1. **Circle.**

1 It's half past four / (half past five)
2 The concert is at half past six / half past seven.
3 Chatter has got a towel. / shampoo.
4 Patty has got a pink towel / a green towel.
5 Patty and Chatter are having a shower / arguing.

I'm Tag.
This is my towel.

Learn with Tag

I	my		it	its
you	your		we	our
he	his		you	your
she	her		they	their

2 **Write.**

1 She's doing .... *her* .... *homework* ....

2 He's riding ....

3 We're reading ....

4 They're sleeping in ....

5 I'm wearing ....

3 **Ask and answer.**

What's the time?

It's half past two.

1   2   3   4

4 **Sing along with the FlyHigh band!** ♫

The bike song
My bike is yellow.
Your bike is blue.
His bike is old.
Her bike is new.
We are on our bikes.
Ride your bikes too!
Where are the animals?
They're in their zoo!
Come and play with us,
Here in our zoo.

14

ready   trumpet   drums   keyboard tambourine

This is Trumpet's trumpet.

1 Are you ready? Have you got your musical instruments?

Yes, here are Chatter's drums.

2 Here is Tag's guitar. This is Karla's keyboard.

Where's my tambourine?

3 This is Trumpet's trumpet!

Whose is this?

It's Patty's tambourine!

Oh, thank you, Rob!

4 Ladies and gentlemen, boys and girls. Here are the Fly High band with their famous song, 'Welcome to our zoo'!

---

1 **Match.**

 a
 b
 c

1 They're my drums.
2 This is my guitar.
3 This is my tambourine.
4 This is my keyboard.
5 This is my trumpet.

 e
 d

Learn with Tag

Whose is this photo? It's Chatter's photo.
This is Tag's head.
These are Trumpet's ears.

2 **Write.**

   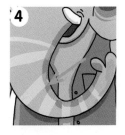  

1 This is ....Patty's head........ .
2 These are ....
3 These are ....

4 This is ....
5 This is ....
6 This is ....

3 **Play the game.**

Whose is this?

It's Anna's ruler!

4 **Write with Karla.**

My friends have got lots of toys. Chatter's bike is blue. Patty's kite is green and white. Tag's rollerblades are black and Trumpet's water pistol is red.

My friends have got lots of toys. ....
....
....
....

15

 orange   thirsty   peach   watermelon   glass   straw  juice

We've got some oranges.

---

1 **Circle.**

1 Vicky is thirsty.   (yes) / no
2 They've got some oranges.   yes / no
3 They haven't got any peaches.   yes / no
4 They've got some watermelons.   yes / no
5 Vicky likes the juice.   yes / no

We've got some oranges.

Learn with Tag

Are there **any** bananas?
Yes, there are **some** bananas.
Have you got **any** peaches?
Yes, we've got **some** peaches.
Have you got **any** apples?
No, we haven't got **any** apples.
There aren't **any** apples.

2 **Write** some **or** any.

1 Have we got _____any_____ oranges?
2 Yes, we've got _____ oranges.
3 Are there _____ watermelons?
4 Yes, there are _____ watermelons.
5 There aren't _____ strawberries.
6 We've got _____ straws.

3 **Match.**

1 There aren't
2 Are there any
3 Have we got
4 We've got some

a any straws?
b glasses.
c any peaches.
d bananas?

4 **Sing along with** the **FlyHigh** band! 🎵

The fruit song
We've got some peaches
Strawberries too.
We've got some cherries
Here in the zoo.
Have we got any juice?
Yes, we're making some just for you.

We've got some apples
And oranges too.
We've got bananas
Here in the zoo.
Have we got any juice?
Yes, we're making some just for you.

 fridge
 water
 flour
 sugar
 butter

There isn't much spaghetti.

(1) **Choose and write.**

milk   ~~spaghetti~~   flour   people

1 There isn't much ___spaghetti___ in the cupboard.
2 There isn't any _____ in the fridge.
3 They've got some _____ for a cake.
4 There aren't many _____ in the supermarket.

Learn with Tag

How many bananas are there?
There are six bananas.

How much water is there?
There isn't much water.

How much spaghetti is there?
There is lots of spaghetti.

How many biscuits are there?
There aren't many biscuits.

2 **Write** much **or** many.

1 How ..... much ..... water is there? There isn't .... water.
2 How .... apples are there? There aren't .... apples.
3 How .... eggs are there? There aren't .... eggs.
4 How .... sugar is there? There isn't .... sugar.

3 **Listen and circle.**

1 There's some cheese / lots of cheese.
2 There are lots of oranges / two oranges.
3 There isn't any butter / much butter.
4 There aren't many cherries / any cherries.

4 **Play the game.**

In my fridge I've got some carrots.

In my fridge I've got some carrots and some cheese.

In my fridge I've got some carrots, some cheese and some butter.

mouse

tomato

1 Look! Four babies! Are they mice?

I'm not sure.

2 I think they're hungry. Let's give th some milk

They're drinking it! They're so sweet!

3 The babies are very big now! Are they foxes?

I'm not sure. They're hungry.

4 Let's give them some tomatoes.

They're eating the They're so sweet!

1 **Read and answer.**

1 How many babies are there?   There are four babies.
2 Are they hungry?
3 What do the babies drink?
4 Are they sheep?
5 What do the babies eat?
6 What are the babies?

sheep
 potato
 wolf
 sandwich

(5) The babies are very big now! Are they sheep?

I'm not sure. They're hungry.

(6) Let's give them some potatoes.

They're eating them. They're so sweet!

(7) The babies aren't babies!

What are they?

They're wolves! They're big wolves!

(8) These sandwiches are delicious!

Thank you very much.

Our pleasure.

(2) **Write with Karla.**

In our fridge at home we've got lots of milk and water. We've got some peaches. We haven't got many eggs. We haven't got much butter. We haven't got any tomatoes.

In our fridge at home we've got

....

....

....

....

....

The FlyHigh Review 4

1 **Choose and write.**

my   your   his   her   its   our   ~~their~~

1 They've got a tree house in _their_ garden.
2 He's wearing .... new shoes.
3 We're taking a photo of .... teacher.
4 Has she got a book in .... bag?

5 The dog is playing with .... ball.
6 I'm having .... breakfast.
7 Are you drinking .... milk?

2 **Read and answer.**

1 Whose bike is it?
It's David's bike.

2 Whose skateboard is it?

3 Whose sunglasses are they?

4 Whose ball is it?

5 Whose guitar is it?

3 **Listen and circle.**

We've got some ...
juice
oranges
butter
cheese
strawberries

We haven't got any ...
juice
oranges
butter
cheese
strawberries

4 **Match.**

a   b    c    d

1 It's half past seven. **2** It's half past eleven. **3** It's half past ten.   **4** It's half past three.

5 Circle and write.

1 How much / (How many) .... are there?

2 How much / How many .... is there?

3 How much / How many 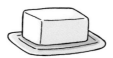 .... is there?

4 How much / How many .... are there?

5 How much / How many .... is there?

6 Write.

1 one tomato   *two tomatoes*
2 one baby   ....
3 one sandwich   ....
4 one wolf   ....

5 one mouse   ....
6 one sheep   ....
7 one potato   ....
8 one strawberry   ....

My Project — Make a food poster.

My breakfast		This is *my* breakfast. There's a bowl of bananas, peaches and strawberries, and some bread and honey. There isn't *much* orange juice in the glass.
My lunch		This is *my* lunch. There's a big sandwich with cheese and tomatoes. There's a glass of water too.
My dinner	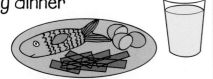	This is *my* dinner. There's a big fish and there are lots of carrots. There aren't many potatoes. There's lots of milk in the glass.

Now go to
My Picture Dictionary

17

 team

 heavy

 throw

 dirty

 draw

Trumpet is stronger.

1 It's the zoo Olympics. There's a red team and a blue team.

That dog can jump very high.

Yes, but Karla is taller. She can jump really high.

2 This is heavy.

Look at Hilda Hippo. She's very strong.

Trumpet is stronger. He can throw a long way.

3 Wow! Chatter is faster than everyone else.

He's dirtier than everyone else!

4 The blue team is fantastic.

The red team is better. Which team is the winner?

It's a draw! Congratulations, everyone.

---

1 **Circle.**

1 There's a red team and a yellow team / blue team.
2 The dog can jump high / climb fast.
3 The hippo is very small / strong.
4 Chatter is dirty / hungry.
5 There is a winner / draw.

Trumpet is stronger than me.

2 **Write.**

1 Elephants are ....stronger............ (strong) than zebras.
2 Hippos are .... (heavy) than frogs.
3 Snakes are .... (long) than mice.
4 Whales are .... (big) than dolphins.
5 Swans are .... (pretty) than vultures.

3 **Listen and stick. Then write.**

Susan   Lucy   Angela   Maria

1 Is Lucy taller than Susan?   Yes, she is.
2 Is Susan shorter than Angela? ....
3 Is Angela dirtier than Maria? ....

4 **Sing along with the FlyHigh band!** 🎵

We're the winners.
We are the blue team, yes, we are.
We are the blue team, yes, we are.
We are better, better than the red.
We are taller, we are faster, yes, we are.
We are bigger, we are stronger, yes, we are.
We are better, better, better than the red.
We're better, better, better than the red team.
We're the winners.
We are the red team …

18

world	rhino	young	giraffe	fat	thin

The best zoo in the world. ♫

It's the end of the zoo Olympics. There's a party and everyone is happy.

1 Girls and boys all over the world
Come and see our fun zoo games.
They make friends with Vicky and Rob
And with the animals too.
It's the best zoo in the world.
It's the best zoo for me and you.

2 The rhino is the funniest.
The mouse is the youngest.
The giraffe is the tallest.
The frog is the smallest.
Everyone is special in their own way.

3 The hippo is the fattest.
The fox is the thinnest.
The snake is the longest.
Trumpet is the strongest.
Everyone is special
in their own way.

4 Animals all over the world
Come and see our fun zoo games.
We make friends with girls and boys.
We make friends with their families too.
It's the best zoo in the world.
It's the best zoo for me and you.

1 **Match.**

1 The giraffe   **a** is young.
2 The rhino   **b** is tall.
3 The mouse   **c** is thin.
4 The hippo   **d** is funny.
5 The fox   **e** is fat.

Tag is the fastest in the zoo.

Learn with Tag

young – younger – the youngest
funny – funnier – the funniest
fat – fatter – the fattest

good – better – the best
bad – worse – the worst

2 **Write.**

1 Rob is ....the cleverest........ (clever) boy.
2 Vicky is .... (pretty) girl.
3 Patty's sister is .... (young) bird.
4 Trumpet is .... (heavy) animal.
5 Tag is .... (good) dancer.
6 Chatter is .... (bad) singer.

3 **Choose and write.**

fast   thin   ~~big~~   dirty   slow

1 Eddie is ....the biggest........ .
2 Adam is ....
3 Carl is ....
4 Rob is ....
5 David is ....

4 **Write with Karla.**

Trumpet is the tallest.
Patty is the shortest.
Pandora is the youngest.
I'm the oldest.
Sally has got the longest hair.

.... the tallest in our class.

cry   nurse   accident   middle   finger

We were in the playground.

① Vicky is crying.

Quick. Where's the nurse?

Here I am.

② What's the matter?

We were in the playground. Chatter was on his rollerblades and Tag was on his bike and there was an accident

And I was in the middle. Look at my fingers.

③ You were lucky. Everything is OK. Karla, please go home with Vicky.

---

1 **Circle.**

1	Vicky is crying.	yes / no
2	Karla is looking for Vicky.	yes / no
3	The nurse looks at Vicky's hand.	yes / no
4	Vicky's fingers are OK.	yes / no
5	Karla and Vicky are going to the playground.	yes / no

On Sunday I was at the zoo.

Learn with Tag

I/He/She/It **was** at the zoo.
You/We/They **were** at the shop.

2 **Write** was **or** were.

Sunday (**1**) ...... *was* ...... hot and sunny. It (**2**) .... a busy day for my family.
My brother (**3**) .... at the zoo with my mum. There (**4**) ....
lots of visitors at the zoo. My dad (**5**) .... at the circus. He's a clown! I
(**6**) .... at a party. My friends (**7**) .... there too.

3 **Choose and write.**

tired ~~hot~~ hungry happy thirsty

1 It was ...... *hot* ....
2 The baby was ....
3 The girl was ....
4 The ducks were ....
5 The boy was ....

4 **Sing along with** the **FlyHigh** band!

There was an accident.
It was a hot afternoon.
I was at the zoo.
I was at the zoo.

I was with all of my friends.
Tag and Chatter were there too.
Tag and Chatter were there too.

Chatter was on his rollerblades.
Tag was on his bike.
Tag was on his bike.

There was an accident
In the playground
But we are all right.
But we are all right.

20

 bandage

 grapes

 ambulance

 yesterday

There weren't any chocolates.

1 Vicky has got a bandage on her hand.

We're sorry.

There weren't any chocolates but we've got some grapes for you.

Thank you.

2 Was there an ambulance?

No, there wasn't.

I don't know. I wasn't there.

3 Was your bike OK yesterday?

Yes, it was.

4 Where are the grapes?

Trumpet!

Sorry, Vicky. I can get you some more.

---

1 **Choose and write.**

ambulance ~~sorry~~ yesterday grapes

1 Tag and Chatter are ....sorry........ .

2 Vicky was in an accident ....

3 Tag and Chatter have got some .... for Vicky.

4 There wasn't an ....

Was your bike OK?

Yes, it was.

Learn with Tag

I/He/She/It wasn't tired.
You/We/They weren't sad.

Was I/he/she/it at home?

Were you/we/they at school?

Yes, I/he/she/it was.
No, I/he/she/it wasn't.
Yes, you/we/they were.
No, you/we/they weren't.

2 **Write** was/wasn't **or** were/weren't.

1 His mum _____was_____ a nurse.
She _____wasn't_____ a teacher.

2 He _____ in bed yesterday.
He _____ at school.

3 They _____ in an ambulance.
They _____ in a car.

4 We _____ at home last night.
We _____ at the party.

3 **Play the game.**

Were you hungry yesterday?

No, I wasn't.

happy   sad
hungry   tired
thirsty excited
bored   brave

Were you tired?

Yes, I was.

This man was a giant. His name was Robert Wadlow. He was American. When he was eight, he was 1 metre and 83 centimetres tall. When he was 22, he was 2 metres and 72 centimetres tall. He was the tallest man in the world. His feet were 47 centimetres long. They were the biggest feet in the world.

This is the biggest flower in the world. It's orange and white. It's 91 centimetres across. You can see these flowers in forests. They aren't very pretty.

This is a hummingbird. It's 57 millimetres long. Hummingbirds are the smallest birds in the world. They can fly and sing. They make the smallest nests in the world. They've got the smallest eggs too.

---

1 **Read and answer.**

1 How long were Robert Wadlow's feet?   They were 47 centimetres long.
2 How big is the flower?
3 How long is the hummingbird?
4 How old was the youngest Olympic winner?
5 How fast can a cheetah run?
6 How big is Lake Baikal?

Marjorie Gestring was a diver. She was the youngest person ever to win a gold medal in the summer Olympics. She was thirteen years and nine months old. She was American.

The cheetah is the fastest animal in the world. It can run 100 kilometres an hour. It's got a small head and four strong legs. It's 80 centimetres tall. It eats meat and it lives in Africa.

Lake Baikal is in Russia. It's the oldest lake in the world. It's also one of the biggest lakes in the world. It's 630 kilometres long and 48 kilometres across. It's the deepest lake and it's one of the clearest lakes in the world too. The water is very clean and a beautiful blue. It's home to many different plants and animals.

2 **Write with Karla.**

<u>My Book of Records</u>
The tallest person I know is Sally.
The oldest person I know is Vicky's grandpa.
The biggest shop I know is the supermarket.
The longest word I know in English is hummingbirds.

<u>My Book of Records</u>

The tallest person I know is

....

....

....

....

....

....

1 Colour.

Animals =

First Aid =

Numbers =

Food =

mouse

eighty

rhino

frog

seventy-two

ambulance

giraffe

thirty-nine

grapes

fox

one hundred

chocolates

sixty-four

strawberries

bandage

nurse

2 Circle.

1 Cars are (faster) / slower than bikes.
2 Girls are older / younger than women.
3 A month is longer / shorter than a year.

4 Giraffes are taller / shorter than rhinos.
5 Summer is colder / hotter than winter.
6 Hippos are fatter / thinner than wolves.

3 Write was/wasn't or were/weren't.

Zeppo   Coco

Pampa

Lenny

1 There ___were___ four clowns.
2 Lenny _____ the smallest.
3 Coco and Zeppo _____ the shortest.

4 Pampa _____ the thinnest.
5 Lenny _____ the fattest.
6 Zeppo _____ the tallest.

4 **Listen and match.**

1 Anna   **2** Betty   **3** Caroline and Denise   **4** Ellie

a

b

c

d

Now ask and answer.

Was she at the cinema?

Was she at the circus?

Was it Anna?

No, she wasn't.

Yes, she was.

Yes, it was.

5 **What about you? Write.**

1 Were you at school on Sunday? ....

2 Was your mum at home last night? ....

3 Was your dad on holiday last month? ....

4 Was it sunny yesterday? ....

5 Were your friends at the park yesterday? ....

My Project   **Make a weather chart.**

Now go to My Picture Dictionary

FUN TIME 2

1 Say it with Sally.

a) Listen and point. Then repeat.

 ph

 ch

 sh

th

b) Listen and write. Then repeat.

1 **3** th ree

2 ....oto

3 ....ark

4 ....air

5 ele.......ant

6 pea.......

7 fi.......

8 tee.......

c) Chant.

A photo of a dolphin.   Three teeth.   Shirts and shorts.   Chatter and the children.

2 Play the word race.

1 three seasons ....spring....... ....

2 three months ....

3 three musical instruments  ....

4 three animals ....

5 three fruits ....

6 three rooms ....

7 three places ....

8 three parts of the body ....

Write.

The best …		The worst …	
drink is		food is	
book is		song is	
month is		sport is	
lesson is		shop is	

 Find. Then ask and answer.

Whose … is it?   Whose … are they?
It's …   They are …

Whose tambourine is it?   It's Lydia's.

tambourine   trumpet   drums   keyboard
sunglasses   hat   swimsuit   towel
bag   watch   sweets   hair slide

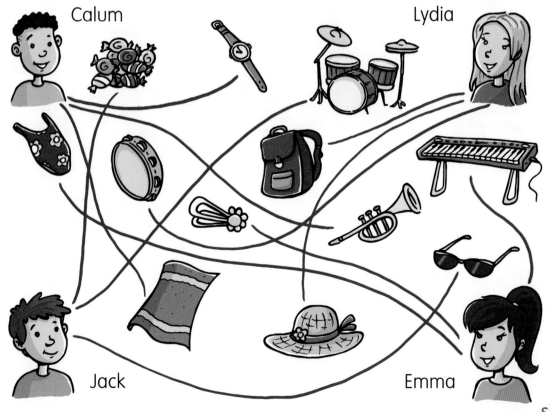

21

reporter photographer work newspaper

We danced in the Olympics.

This is Julie and this is Brad. She's a reporter and he's a photographer. They work for a newspaper, News 4U.

This is Karla. She was in the red team.

Karla, you jumped ten metres in the zoo Olympics.

Yes, that's right!

Tag played basketball with the blue team.

We climbed and walked and danced in the Olympics. They were great!

1 Match.

1 She's a reporter.
2 He's a photographer.
3 It's a newspaper.
4 She was in the red team.
5 He was in the blue team.

a Karla
b News 4U
c Julie
d Tag
e Brad

Yesterday I played basketball.

Monday	
Tuesday	Today
Wednesday	
Thursday	
Friday	
Saturday	
Sunday	

Learn with Tag

clean	cleaned	paint	painted
climb	climbed	play	played
dance	danced	talk	talked
help	helped	visit	visited
listen	listened	watch	watched

2 **Choose and write.**

1 Yesterday we ....watched.... TV.

2 Yesterday I .... the tallest tree in the garden.

3 Yesterday he .... his guitar.

4 Yesterday they .... their aunt and uncle.

5 Yesterday she .... to some songs.

play   visit   ~~watch~~

climb   listen

3 **Listen and stick. Then circle.**

Monday	Tuesday	Wednesday

1 On Monday she danced in / (cleaned) her bedroom.

2 On Tuesday she helped / visited her aunt and uncle.

3 On Wednesday she helped / painted her dad.

4 **Sing along with the FlyHigh band!** ♫

I was at school.

Yesterday I walked to school
And I talked to all my friends.
Yesterday I was at school
And I played with all my friends.

We climbed, we jumped, we played basketball.
We liked our day at our lovely school!

Yesterday I walked to school
And I laughed with all my friends.
Yesterday I was at school
I was happy with my friends.

22

clean up

wet

Did you wash the floor, Sally?

1) **Circle.**

1 There was an accident / a party.
2 The animals cleaned up the paint / mess.
3 They helped Sally / Chatter.
4 Sally washed the dishes / floor.
5 The floor is dirty / wet.

Learn with Tag

Did I/he/she/it play?

Yes, I/he/she/it did.
No, I/he/she/it didn't.

Did you/we/they play?

Yes, you/we/they did.
No, you/we/they didn't.

2 **Look and answer.**
My family yesterday

1 Did Grandma play the guitar?
No, she didn't.

2 Did Grandma play the drums?

3 Did Grandpa watch TV?

4 Did Dad skip?

5 Did Mum play the drums?

3 **Ask and answer. Say** Yes, I did **or** No, I didn't.

Did you play football yesterday?

Did you wash your face this morning?

Did you listen to music yesterday?

Did you clean your teeth this morning?

4 **Write with Karla.**

Dear Kevin,
How are you? I've got lots of questions for you!
Did you play tennis yesterday?
Did you clean your bedroom?
Did you wash your dad's car?
Did you watch TV?
With love from
Karla

Dear ....,

....

....

....

....

....

....

23

mayor

proud

We had a wonderful time.

1 **Choose and write.**

holiday   mayor   ~~newspaper~~   prize

1 There's a photo of the animals in the ___newspaper___ .
2 The _____ comes to see the animals.
3 He's got a _____ for the animals.
4 The prize is a _____ in Turkey.

I went to school yesterday.

Monday
Tuesday
Wednesday
Thursday
Friday
Saturday   Today
Sunday

Learn with Tag

buy	bought	go	went
come	came	have	had
do	did	read	read
drink	drank	see	saw
eat	ate	take	took
give	gave	write	wrote

2 **Write.**

1 We drink milk every morning. We ......*drank*...... milk yesterday.

2 The children read books every week. They .... three books last week.

3 My mum takes lots of photos. She .... a good photo last Sunday.

4 My dad eats lots of oranges. He .... an orange this morning.

5 I see my friends every day. I .... my friends yesterday.

3 **Match.**

1 We ate —   **a** to the beach.
2 I drank   **b** a handstand.
3 They read   **c** their English books.
4 My sister did   **d** three sandwiches.
5 You went   **e** some apple juice.

4 **Sing along with the FlyHigh band!** ♫

Wonderful dreams

I didn't play with my friends.
I didn't go to the park.
I didn't play with my friends.
No no, no no, no no.
I sat in my room
And read my books.
I had a wonderful time
With my friends in my books.

Oh yes, I played in my head
And I had wonderful dreams.
Dreams of so many things.
Oh yes, I did, oh yes.
I read all of my books
Last weekend.

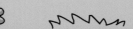

 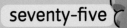

24

flippers

sun cream

phone

Did you drink your milk?

1 **Circle.**

1 The suitcases are ready.   (yes) / no
2 The animals have got their flippers. yes / no
3 They had lunch.   yes / no
4 Rob and Vicky were sad.   yes / no

Did you go to school yesterday?
Yes, I did. / No, I didn't.

2 **What about you? Write.**

1 Did you have a shower last night? ....
2 Did you have breakfast this morning? ....
3 Did your friends come to your house yesterday? ....
4 Did you go to bed at nine o'clock last night? ....
5 Did you eat some fruit yesterday? ....

3 **Listen and circle.**

1 Did they go to the beach?   Yes, they did. / No, they didn't.
2 Did they swim?   Yes, they did. / No, they didn't.
3 Did the boy have an ice cream? Yes, he did. / No, he didn't.
4 Did the girl see a crab?   Yes, she did. / No, she didn't.

4 **Play the game.**

I saw an animal. It was black and white.

Did you see a panda?

No, I didn't.

Did you see a zebra?

Yes, I did!

Sally's Story

A week in London

1st first   2nd second   3rd third

1 Last summer Sam and Katie went on holiday to London. They went for a week.

2 On the first day they visited Buckingham Palace. They didn't see the Queen!

3 On the second day they went to Hyde Park. They played in the boats, but they didn't swim in the Serpentine Lake. It was very cold.

4 On the third day they saw Big Ben. The time was eight o'clock.

---

1 **Read and answer.**

1 Where did Sam and Katie go last summer? _They went to London._

2 Which palace did they visit? ....

3 What did they see on the third day? ....

4 When did they go on the London Eye? ....

5 What did they do on the sixth day? ....

6 What did they buy on the last day? ....

fourth　　fifth　　sixth　　last

(5) On the fourth day they went to the Natural History Museum. They liked the dinosaurs and they bought some postcards.

(6) On the fifth day they went on the London Eye. They saw all the city and the River Thames. It was a beautiful sunny day and they were very excited.

(7) On the sixth day they went to Madame Tussaud's Museum. They saw all the famous people. Prince William was their favourite.

(8) On the last day they went shopping in Oxford Street. They bought presents for their friends and some new clothes. They had a wonderful time in London.

2 **Write with Karla.**

Dear Sally,
I went to London.
I visited a museum.
I bought some presents.
I liked Hyde Park best.
I had a wonderful time.
Love
Karla

Dear .... ,

....

....

....

....

....

The FlyHigh Review 6

1 Write.

1 play _played_
2 walk ....
3 listen ....

4 climb ....
5 clean ....
6 help ....

2 Match.

1 go
2 see
3 have
4 take
5 eat
6 drink

a saw
b took
c ate
d drank
e went
f had

3 Write.

1 I drank milk. I _didn't drink_ orange juice.
2 I ate cake. I .... cheese.
3 I had breakfast. I .... lunch.
4 I went to the circus. I .... to the cinema.
5 I took a photo of my sister. I .... a photo of my brother.
6 I saw a fox. I .... a bear.

4 Read and answer.

Last weekend Rob and Vicky went to the park. Rob played football with his friends and Vicky did handstands. They ate some sandwiches and drank some water. They walked home.

1 Did Rob and Vicky go to the park? _Yes, they did._
2 Did Rob play football? ....
3 Did Vicky ride her bike? ....
4 Did they eat biscuits? ....
5 Did they drink water? ....
6 Did they go home by bus? ....

5 Listen and circle.

1 They (went) / didn't go to Paris.
2 They went / didn't go on a boat.
3 They swam / didn't swim in the river.
4 Their dad bought / didn't buy some sunglasses.

6 Ask and answer. Say Yes, I did or No, I didn't.

Yesterday …
1 Did you drink chocolate milk? ....
2 Did you phone a friend? ....
3 Did you play a computer game? ....
4 Did you eat a sandwich? ....
5 Did you read a good book? ....

My Project   Make a picture diary.

On Sunday I visited my grandparents.
Sunday
On Monday I played basketball.
Monday
Tuesday
On Tuesday I climbed in the playground.
Wednesday
On Wednesday I read a book.
Thursday
On Thursday I ate two oranges.
On Friday I saw a butterfly.
Friday
On Saturday I phoned my friends.
Saturday

Now go to My Picture Dictionary

25

 sandcastle armbands bucket spade sun

Can we make a sandcastle?

1 Sally and the animals go to the beach.

Welcome to Turkey.

Hello, Ziggy!

2 I've got my armbands on. Can we go in the sea?

Yes, you can.

Can I have an ice cream?

No, you can't. Not now.

3 Can we make a sandcastle? We've got our buckets and spades.

You can make a sandcastle under the umbrella. The sun is very hot.

4 You're pink and black!

I know! I didn't wear my sun cream on Monday.

---

1 **Choose and write.**

~~beach~~   sun cream   armbands   buckets and spades

1 Sally and the animals go to the ......beach...... .

2 Karla is wearing her ....

3 Tag and Trumpet have got their ....

4 Ziggy didn't wear his ....

Can I go to the bathroom, please?

Yes, you can.

Learn with Tag

Can you eat in bed?	Yes, I can.
Can he come to the party?	Yes, he can.
Can she go home now?	No, she can't.
Can we have some ice cream, please?	Yes, you can.
Can you ride your bikes at school?	No, we can't.
Can they play football in the living room?	No, they can't.

2 **Listen and stick.**

1

2

3

4

3 **What about you? Circle.**

1 Can you eat in your classroom?   Yes, we can. / No, we can't.
2 Can you jump on your bed at home?   Yes, I can. / No, I can't.
3 Can you play football in your living room? Yes, I can. / No, I can't.
4 Can your friends come and play at your house? Yes, they can. / No, they can't.

4 **Sing along with the FlyHigh band!**

Can I ...?
Can I play with my friends, please?
Can I go and climb those trees?
Can I play with my friends, please?
Yes, you can.

Do your homework, write and read.
Do your English homework, please.
Then you can climb the trees.
Yes, you can.

You can go and play outside.
Please be home by half past five.
You can have a lovely time.
Yes, you can.

26

worried

far

stay

near

scared

stuck

monster

You must be brave.

1 Sally is worried. Patty isn't wearing armbands.

Look, Sally. I'm swimming.

Patty! You mustn't swim far. You must stay near the beach.

2 Patty is scared.

Help!

What's the matter, Patty?

There's a monster in the sea!

3 Carrie Caretta is stuck.

I'm not a monster! I'm a turtle. I'm Carrie Caretta. I can't move.

4 Everyone wants to help Carrie.

You must be brave, Carrie. You mustn't cry.

We must help Carrie.

---

1 **Circle.**

1 Sally is swimming in the sea.   yes / no

2 There's a big turtle in the sea.   yes / no

3 Carrie Carretta can't move.   yes / no

4 Patty is crying.   yes / no

5 The animals want to help Carrie.   yes / no

You must look left and right.

LEFT   RIGHT

Learn with Tag

I must clean my teeth every day.
You must drink lots of water.
He must do his homework.
We mustn't eat ice cream for breakfast.
You mustn't run in school.

2 **Write** must **or** mustn't.

1 They ___mustn't___ play football here.
2 The car .... stop.

3 She .... look left and right.
4 He .... run across the road.

3 **Write with Karla.**

In our school we must listen to
....
....
....
....
....
....
....
....
....

In our zoo we must listen to Sally.
We mustn't play basketball in the bedroom!
We must do our homework.
We must clean our teeth.
We mustn't make a mess.

27

 safe   fisherman   ask   save

You're safe with us, Carrie.

1 Everyone wants to help Carrie but it's too far.

Look. There are some fishermen. They've got a boat. Let's ask them.

2 Can you help us, please?

Yes, we can help you.

3 Rob! Vicky! Be careful.

4 We've got her.

You're safe with us, Carrie.

You saved me! Thank you.

1. **Read and answer.**

1 Why can't the children help Carrie?   It's too far.
2 Who do they see? ....
3 What have the fishermen got? ....
4 Who saves Carrie? ....

I like you.
You like me.

Learn with Tag

I'm here. Come with me!
You're are my best friend. I love you.
He's very tall. Look at him.
She's fun. I like her.
It's a dog. Can you hear it?
We're going to a party. Come with us.
You're under the table. I can see you.
They're funny clowns. I like them.

2 Choose and write.

me   you   them   it   him   her

1 I'm playing tennis. Look at ....me...... .
2 He's funny. Look at ....
3 She's in the boat. Can you see .... ?
4 They're swimming. Can you see .... ?
5 My school is great. I like ....
6 You're very sweet. I like ....

3 Circle.

1 Look at me and my friend. Look at her / us.
2 Can I take the dog for a walk? Can I take them / it to the park?
3 The shoes are under the table. Can you see them / him?
4 Where's my sun cream? Have you got her / it?
5 Sarah is my best friend. I sit next to her / them at school.
6 I can't do my homework. Can you help it / me?

4 Sing along with the FlyHigh band! ♫

Best friends forever
My friends are funny.
My friends are cool.
I like all my friends at school.
I like them and they like me.
We have fun and we're happy.
We're BFF! We're BFF!
We're Best Friends Forever!

meet

dive

We'll meet again.

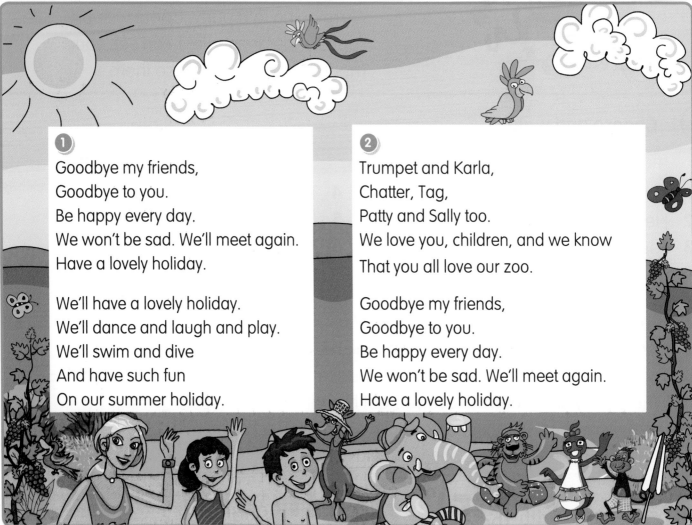

①

Goodbye my friends,
Goodbye to you.
Be happy every day.
We won't be sad. We'll meet again.
Have a lovely holiday.

We'll have a lovely holiday.
We'll dance and laugh and play.
We'll swim and dive
And have such fun
On our summer holiday.

②

Trumpet and Karla,
Chatter, Tag,
Patty and Sally too.
We love you, children, and we know
That you all love our zoo.

Goodbye my friends,
Goodbye to you.
Be happy every day.
We won't be sad. We'll meet again.
Have a lovely holiday.

① **Circle the activities in the song.**

1

2

3

4

5

6

7

8

I'm nine. Next year I'll be ten.

Learn with Tag

In August we'll be on holiday.
We won't go to school.

2 **What about you? Write** I'll **or** I won't.

1 .... go to school in August.
2 .... go to school in September.
3 .... do homework in summer.

4 .... swim in the sea.
5 .... be nine next year.
6 .... eat ice cream in summer.

3 **Listen and circle.**

1 Sandy will / won't go on holiday with her family.
2 She will / won't get up at seven o'clock.
3 She will / won't play volleyball on the beach.
4 She will / won't stay on the beach all day.
5 She will / won't read some books this summer.
6 She will / won't go out in the evening.

4 **Play the game.**

When I grow up I'll be a footballer.

When I grow up I'll be a doctor.

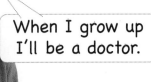

Sally's Story

Our beautiful world

litter

desert

camel

---

1 **Read and answer.**

1 Where does the girl want to go? .... All around the world.
2 What is the first place they see? ....
3 What do they see in the jungle? ....
4 Where is the snow? ....
5 Where is the whale? ....
6 Who must look after the world? ....

jungle

parrot

snow

ocean

(5) Wow! A jungle, parrots and monkeys.

Amazing! It's rainy here.

(6) Mountains and snow!

Incredible! It's cold here.

(7) An ocean and a whale!

Fantastic! It's cloudy here.

(8) You were right, Nelly. We must look after our beautiful world.

(2) **Write with Karla.**

In August I'll be on holiday.
I'll go to the beach.
I won't go to school.
I'll eat watermelons and ice creams.
In September I'll go to school and I'll see my friends again.

In .... I'll be on holiday.

....

....

....

....

....

1 Match.

1 Can I go to the bathroom, please?

2 Can I have some juice, please?

3 Can I ride my bike here?

4 Can I watch TV now?

a

b

c

d

2 What about you? Write Yes, I can or No, I can't.

1 Can you eat in your classroom? ....

2 Can you write on your desk? ....

3 Can you have a mobile phone at school? ....

4 Can you play volleyball in your bedroom? ....

3 Write must or mustn't.

1 We ____must____ drink water every day.

2 Babies .... drink milk.

3 We .... play ball near cars.

4 We .... fight at school.

5 We .... help old people.

6 Babies .... eat chocolate.

4 Choose and write.

~~her~~   him   them   it   us   me

1 Look at Sally. Look at __her__ .

2 I like strawberries. I like ....

3 Can you help me and my friend?
  Can you help .... ?

4 That flower is lovely. Look at ....

5 Where is George? I can't see ....

6 I am going to the park.
  Come with .... !

5 **Listen and match.**

1
Emily

2
Billy

3
Sandra

4
Nick

a

b

c

d

Now write.

1 Emily thinks she .... *will be a dancer* .

2 Billy thinks he ....

3 Sandra thinks she ....

4 Nick thinks he ....

My Project **Make a school rules poster.**

 School rules

We must...
read our books
listen to our teacher
look after our school
help our friends

We mustn't...
play football in class
throw litter
run in the school
fight with our friends

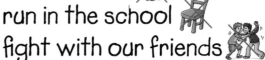

Now go to
My Picture
Dictionary

FUN TIME 3

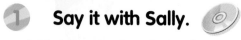

1 Say it with Sally.

a) Listen and point. Then repeat.

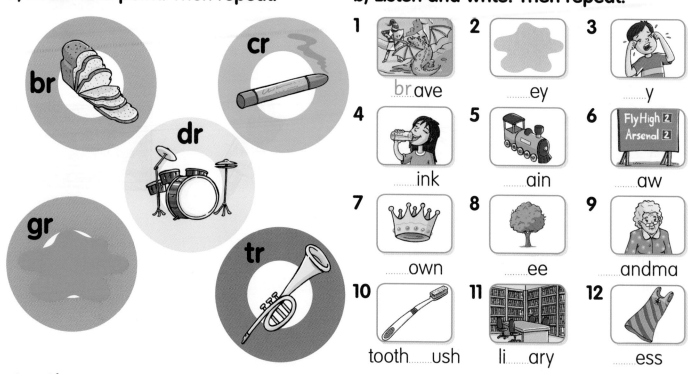

br

cr

dr

gr

tr

b) Listen and write. Then repeat.

1 br.ave

2 ....ey

3 ....y

4 ....ink

5 ....ain

6 ....aw

7 ....own

8 ....ee

9 ....andma

10 tooth....ush

11 li....ary

12 ....ess

c) Chant.

Bread for breakfast.   A crown on a crab.   A dress in a drawer.
Grandma and grandpa.   A trumpet on a train.

2 Find and write the message.

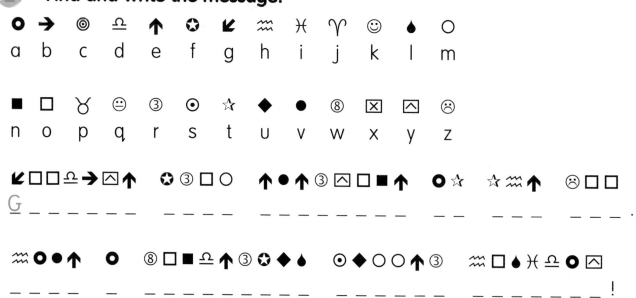

◉	→	◎	♎	↑	✪	↙	≋	⌘	♈	☺	♦	○
a	b	c	d	e	f	g	h	i	j	k	l	m

■	□	♉	☹	③	⊙	☆	◆	●	⑧	⊠	⌂	☹
n	o	p	q	r	s	t	u	v	w	x	y	z

↙ □ □ ♎ → ⌂ ↑   ✪ ③ □ ○   ↑ ● ↑ ③ ⌂ □ ■ ↑   ◉ ☆   ☆ ≋ ↑   ☹ □ □

G _

≋ ◉ ● ↑   ◉   ⑧ □ ■ ♎ ↑ ③ ✪ ◆ ♦   ⊙ ◆ ○ ○ ↑ ③   ≋ □ ♦ ⌘ ♎ ◉ ⌂

_ !

Now write your own message.

3 Do the Fly High Quiz!

1
twenty, thirty,
.... ,
....

2
first, second,
.... ,
....

3
Who was
Julie?

4
Who was
Brad?

5
Yesterday we
....
the tree.

16
What did
Trumpet and
Tag make on
the beach?

15
Which friend
did the
animals meet
in Turkey?

17 You must go
....

6
Yesterday we
....
TV.

7
What did
Tag do in the
Olympics?

14 Did she wear
armbands?

20
Who did Rob
save?

19
What did the
fishermen
have?

18 You must go
....

8
What did
Karla do in the
Olympics?

13 Did he wear
flippers?

12
Where did the
animals go on
holiday?

11
What prize did
the animals
win?

10
Every day
I do my homework.
Yesterday I
.... my
homework.

9
Every day I go to
school. Yesterday
I ....
to school.

 pupil

 school uniform

 gym

 gymnastics

 canteen

cook

Read with Trumpet

A day at school

1 This is a school in Britain. It's nine o'clock in the morning and the pupils are in class. Look at their clothes. It's their school uniform. Pupils in Britain wear uniforms to school every day.

2 It's eleven o'clock and the pupils have got PE. They're in the gym. In PE pupils do many things, like run, play football and do gymnastics. They wear special clothes for PE. What colour are his shorts and T-shirt?

3 It's one o'clock. It's time for lunch now and the children are hungry. They have lunch in the canteen. The cook, Mrs Smith, has got lots of delicious food to eat.

4 It's two o'clock. Mary has got Art. It's her favourite lesson. 'Paint a picture,' says the teacher. Mary is very good at painting and her picture is excellent. Look at all the colours!

1 **Talk about your school day.**

1 What clothes do you wear to school?
2 Have you got PE today?
3 What colour are your PE clothes?
4 Where do you eat lunch?
5 Have you got Art today?
6 What's your favourite lesson?

2 **Write about your school day.**

Today we've got Maths and English.

We haven't got PE.

My favourite lesson is History.

 give
 spider
 lantern
 pumpkin
 bonfire
 fireworks

Read with Trumpet

Special days in Britain

1 Mother's Day is in March. Children give flowers, chocolates and presents to their mothers. They give them beautiful cards too. Children say 'Happy Mother's Day. I love you, Mum.'

2 Harvest Festival is in September. Children put apples, oranges and bananas in pretty boxes. They sing songs at school and say 'Thank you. We've got a lot of food and we aren't hungry.'

3 Halloween is in October. It's fun on this night. Children have parties and wear funny clothes. They dress up as ghosts, spiders and clowns. They eat sweets and cakes and they make lanterns from big pumpkins.

4 Bonfire Night is in November. Children play and put a doll called a 'Guy' on a big bonfire. They watch beautiful fireworks too. It's cold in November and children drink hot soup.

1 **Circle.**

1 Children dress up as ghosts on Mother's Day. yes / no

2 Harvest Festival is in September. yes / no

3 Children put fruit in boxes on Bonfire Night. yes / no

4 Children give cards on Mother's Day. yes / no

5 Bonfire Night is in November. yes / no

6 Halloween is in March. yes / no

2 **Write about special days in your country.**

New Year is in January. We have a party at New Year.

Father's Day is in June. We give cards to our dad on this day.

Christmas is in December. We get presents at Christmas.

 restaurant
 film
 statue
 shell
 sell

Read with Trumpet

A British town centre

① This is a town in Britain. It's Saturday and lots of people are visiting the shopping mall. There are shops and restaurants here. You can go shopping in the mall and you can eat and drink too. You can watch films in the cinema.

② It's great in the town museum! You can see lots of interesting things like toys, trains, animals and paintings. You can also see beautiful statues. This girl is learning about shells.

③ There's a market in the town. There are people selling many things. You can buy fish, apples, oranges and bananas. You can buy clothes, books and watches in the market too.

④ These children are in the library. It's quiet in the library. There are lots of books here and computers too. The children can take books home for a month. Some children are doing homework.

1 **What can you do in these places? Write.**

1 shopping mall: You can go shopping.
2 library: ....
3 museum: ....
4 market: ....
5 cinema: ....

2 **Write about your town.**

In my town, there is a big park. You can play and ride bikes in the park.

There is also a shopping mall in my town. You can buy clothes and have lunch there.

 cereal

 tea

 salt

 vinegar

 pudding

 custard

Read with Trumpet

Food in Britain

1 It's morning and this family is having breakfast. In Britain people sometimes have cereal and fruit in the morning. Other people have eggs and toast or bread and honey. People often drink orange juice or tea with milk.

2 People in Britain love this food, fish and chips! There are many shops across the country. Lots of people put salt and vinegar on the chips. Lovely!

3 This is Sunday lunch! Sometimes people have chicken, potatoes and lots of vegetables. There's often a big pudding with custard too. Custard is sweet and yellow. Many people go for a walk after lunch.

4 On special days we eat special food. At Easter children eat hot cross buns. At Christmas they eat Christmas cake. There's fruit in the buns and the cake. On Pancake Day they eat pancakes. Children like honey or chocolate on their pancakes.

1 **Write** yes **or** no.

1 People drink tea with orange juice. ...no...
2 You can have vinegar with your chips. ....
3 Children eat hot cross buns at Easter. ....
4 People eat custard with chicken. ....
5 Some people have fruit for breakfast. ....
6 There aren't many fish and chip shops in Britain. ....

2 **Write about the food you like.**

For breakfast I like eggs, toast and apple juice.

On Sundays we have spaghetti with cheese.

On my birthday we eat cake and ice cream.

My favourite food is pizza.

 journey hill dry hotel  cave

Read with Trumpet

Amazing holidays

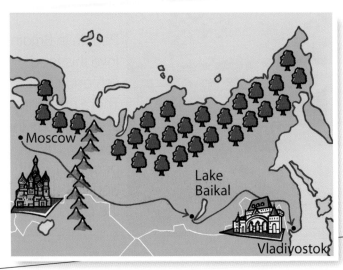

Hi Thomas,

We're in Russia. It's really big – it's the biggest country in the world. We're on the Trans-Siberian train from Moscow to Vladivostok. It's the longest train journey in the world. It takes seven days. Everyone on the train is very friendly. Outside there's snow everywhere. It's much colder than Britain. At the moment I can see some mountains. They're much taller than the hills near my house. They're beautiful. I'm really enjoying this holiday.

Ellie

Hello Natasha,

I'm on holiday in Göreme, a town in Turkey, with my family. It's sunny all the time. It's much hotter here than in Britain. There isn't much rain and there aren't many trees. Everything is very dry. Britain is much wetter and greener. We're staying in the best hotel in the town. It's amazing. Our room is in a cave and it's got a lovely swimming pool. It's smaller than the pool at school, but it's warm and we swim every day.

Laura

1 **Circle.**

1 Russia is the largest country in the world.
yes / no

2 Britain is warmer than Russia. yes / no

3 The hotel is the worst in town. yes / no

4 Turkey is hotter than Britain. yes / no

5 The mountains in Britain are smaller than those in Russia. yes / no

6 Britain is drier than Turkey. yes / no

2 **Write a comparison of your country and Britain.**

My country is Russia. It's much bigger than Britain. My country is the biggest in the world.

Britain is warmer than my country. My country is one of the coldest in the world.

boat

island

carriage

building

1,000,000
one million

1,000
one thousand

Read with Trumpet

A week in New York

Last year I went to New York with my mum and dad. These are my photos.

One day we took a boat to Staten Island. The view of New York was amazing. On the way we saw the Statue of Liberty. It was green and more than 93 metres tall. The French people gave the statue to the Americans in 1886. It was a present for America's 100th birthday. It was ten years late!

Central Park was very big. It was sunny and there were lots of people in the park. We had lunch next to the Lake and watched some people in boats. Then we went for a ride in a horse and carriage.

My family also visited the Empire State Building. Millions of people visit the building every year. It opened on May 1st 1931. It was the tallest building in the world at that time. We went up to the top, and there were wonderful views. The Empire State Building has got 6,500 windows – that's a lot of windows to clean!

On our last day we went shopping on Fifth Avenue. It's one of the most famous shopping streets in the world. I bought a present for my best friend. I got him a T-shirt with an American flag on it.

1 **Talk about a city you visited.**

1 Where did you go?
2 What famous buildings were there in the city?
3 Were there any parks?
4 Were there any statues?
5 Did you go shopping? Where did you go?

2 **Write about a city you visited.**

I visited New York City last summer. We went to the Bronx Zoo. There were many amazing animals.

We also saw the Hudson River. It was very big. My favourite building was the Metropolitan Museum of Art. It was so beautiful!

 hospital   sick   medicine   magazine   fire station   ladder

Read with Trumpet

People in my community

1

This is Doctor Wells. She works at the hospital with other doctors and nurses. She helps sick children. She looks at their eyes and ears. She listens to their hearts. Sometimes Doctor Wells gives medicine to the children to make them better. She likes helping people.

2

Miss Adams is a librarian. She works at the library in the town centre. As well as books, there are DVDs, magazines and newspapers in the library. Miss Adams uses a computer and helps people look for books. She reads stories to children too.

3

This is Mr Brown. He's a firefighter. He works at the fire station with other firefighters. They work in a team. They save people in fires and help people in car accidents. They're very brave. Sometimes Mr Brown climbs a tall ladder and helps cats in trees.

4

Mr Walker is a bus driver. He drives a school bus. It can carry 51 people. Every morning he gets up early and drives the children to school. He must go back to school at the end of the day and take them home again. He drives the same way every day.

1 **Choose and write.**

bus driver   librarian   ~~firefighter~~   doctor

1 A ___firefighter___ works in a fire station.
2 A _____ takes children to school.
3 A _____ reads stories to children.
4 A _____ gives medicine to children.

2 **Write about people in your community.**

Mrs Simpson is a teacher. She works in my school. She teaches English.

Mrs Jones is a doctor. She works in a hospital. She helps sick people.

Mr Green is a librarian. He works in a library. He helps people find books.

 plant   waste   grow  bath   ugly   bin

Read with Trumpet

Looking after our world

①  We must look after the forests. More than half the world's plants and animals live in forests. Many medicines come from these plants. We need forests, but all around the world, people are cutting down trees. They use the trees to make paper and furniture. You can help save the forests. Don't waste paper.

②  People, animals and plants need clean water. We drink water and we wash with it. Plants must have water to grow. We must look after the lakes and rivers. We mustn't waste water. Turn off the water when you clean your teeth. Baths use more water than showers. Take a shower, not a bath.

③  We must look after our towns and keep them clean. People don't like dirty streets – they're ugly. Children can't play in playgrounds with a lot of litter – they can have accidents. You can help. Don't throw litter in the park or the street. Take it home or put it in a bin.

④  We need clean air. Dirty air makes people sick. In 1952 many people got very sick in London because the air was dirty. Today London's air is much cleaner but cars still make it dirty. You can help. Don't always go by car. Walk or ride a bike.

① **Tick (✓) the good actions and cross (✗) the bad actions.**

1 throw litter in the bin ....✓........
2 waste paper ....
3 save water ....
4 ride a bike ....
5 drop litter ....
6 always go by car ....

② **Write about how you can help the world.**

I can ride a bike to school. This helps keep the air clean.

I must throw litter in the bin. Dirty cities are ugly.

I mustn't waste water. We need water to live.

All:	Hello!
Sally:	Hello!
Child 1	
(to Sally):	Hello! Are you English?
Sally:	Yes, I am. My name's Sally and I'm from England.
All:	My name's …
All:	We're from …
All sing:	Let's dance! (Lesson 1)
Sally:	These are my friends: Chatter, Trumpet, Tag, Karla and Patty.
Animals:	Hello! We're the animals in the zoo!
Child 2:	Do you go to school?
Chatter:	Yes, we do. Do you?
Children:	Yes, we do!
All sing:	Lucky girls and boys (Lesson 3)
Patty:	Did you go to school yesterday?
Child 3:	Yes, we did.
All sing:	I was at school. (Lesson 21)
Trumpet:	I'm hungry!
Animals:	You're always hungry, Trumpet!
Children 4 & 5:	We're making a cake!

Music Show

All sing: Fun in the kitchen (Lesson 9)

Child 5: That cake was delicious! Now I'm thirsty. Have we got any juice?

Animals: Yes, we have!

All sing: The fruit song (Lesson 15)

Tag: Can we go out and play now, Sally?

Sally: You must do your homework first.

All sing: Can I …? (Lesson 25)

Karla: Let's play! Let's have two teams.

All sing: We're the winners. (Lesson 17)

All sing: The best zoo in the world. (Lesson 18)

Sally: You are all winners!

Patty: We are all friends!

All sing: Best friends forever (Lesson 27)

Sally: It's summer and we don't go to school in summer.

All: Hooray!

Sally: What do we do in summer?

All: We go on holiday!

All sing: We'll meet again. (Lesson 28)

Listen, point and say. Then write.

1

....

    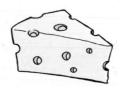

....

....

....

 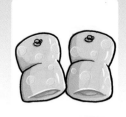  

 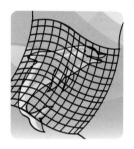